INVESTING MADE EASY FOR KIDS: A
BEGINNER'S GUIDE TO FINANCIAL SUCCESS

Contents

Chapter 1. Introduction to Investing

Why Learn about Investing?

Imagine you have a magical tool that can help your money grow while you sleep. This magical tool is called investing. Learning about investing is like unlocking the secrets to making your money work for you, so you can achieve your dreams and goals faster.

As a kid, you might think investing is something only grown-ups do, but that is not true. Learning about investing from a young age can give you a head start on building a secure financial future. When you understand how money grows through investments, you'll have the knowledge to make smart choices with your money as you grow up.

Investing is not just about making money; it is also about learning important life skills. It teaches you how to set goals, make thoughtful decisions, and be patient. So, whether you want to buy your favourite toys, go on exciting adventures, or save up for a big goal like college, learning about investing can help you get there.

What is Investing?

Investing is a bit like planting seeds in a garden. When you plant seeds and take care of them, they grow into beautiful plants. Similarly, when you invest money, you're putting it into things that have the potential to grow and become more valuable over time.

In the world of investing, your "seeds" are your money, and the "garden" is the various ways you can put that money to work. These ways include stocks, bonds, mutual funds, real estate, and more. Each of these options comes with its own level of risk and potential for growth.

For example, when you invest in stocks, you're buying tiny pieces of a company. If the company does well and makes more money, the value of your stock can increase. But if the company faces challenges, the value can go down too. Bonds, on the other hand, involve lending money to governments or companies, and they pay you back with interest over time. Each type of investment has its own rules and potential rewards.

The Power of Compound Interest

Have you heard the phrase "Time is money"? Well, when it comes to investing, time can actually make your money grow bigger. This magical growth is thanks to something called compound interest.

Imagine you have a piggy bank with $100 in it, and it earns an interest rate of 10% per year. After the first year, you'll have $110, right? But here's where it gets exciting: in the second year, you'll earn interest not just on your initial $100, but also on the $10 you earned in the first year. So, you'll earn $11 in interest, bringing your total to $121.

As the years go by, this cycle continues. You earn interest not only on your original money but also on the interest you've already earned. This snowball effect is what makes compound interest so powerful. The longer your money stays invested, the more it can grow exponentially.

Imagine you start investing as a kid and keep investing a little bit each month. By the time you're a young adult, your money could have grown significantly. This growth is thanks to the power of compound interest working its magic over time.

Understanding the basics of investing, like compound interest, gives you an advantage in making informed decisions about your money. While it might seem complex at first, learning step by step will make you a savvy investor in no time.

Chapter 2. Setting the Foundation

Money Basics: Earning, Saving, and Spending

Before you dive into the exciting world of investing, it is important to understand the basics of how money works. Money is not just something you spend; it's a tool that can help you achieve your dreams. To use this tool wisely, you need to know how to earn, save, and spend your money.

Earning money might sound like something only adults do, but even kids can find ways to earn a little extra cash. You could help with chores around the house, walk dogs for neighbours, or even start a small business like selling lemonade or crafts. Earning money teaches you the value of hard work and shows you that money does not come for free.

Once you have money in your pocket, it is time to think about saving. Saving means putting a portion of your money aside for later. When you save, you are giving yourself the opportunity to make bigger plans and reach your goals. Having a savings goal, like buying a new toy or saving up for a trip, can motivate you to set money aside regularly.

Spending is the part of money management that often gets the most attention. It is fun to spend money on things you like, but it's also important to be smart about it. Before you spend, ask yourself if it is something you really need or if it's just something you want. Learning to make thoughtful spending choices is a key skill that will serve you well as you start investing.

The Importance of Goals

Imagine you are going on a treasure hunt. What is the first thing you need? A map, right? Well, in the world of money, goals are like your treasure map. They guide you towards where you want to go.

Setting financial goals is like deciding where you want to find your treasure. Your goals could be short-term (things you want to achieve soon) or long-term (things that might take a while). Short-term goals might include buying a new toy or going on a special outing. Long-term goals could be saving for college or even buying your own house when you grow up.

When you have clear goals, it is easier to make smart decisions about your money. For example, if you are saving up for a new bike, you will think twice before spending your money on something else. Goals give you a reason to save and invest, helping you stay focused on the bigger picture.

Differentiating Between Needs and Wants

Imagine you are at a store, and you see a shiny new toy that you really want. It is natural to feel excited, but before you make a decision, take a moment to think: Do you really need it, or is it something you want?

Needs are things that you cannot live without, like food, clothes, and a safe place to live. Wants, on the other hand, are things that you would like to have, but they are not necessary for survival. Learning to tell the difference between needs and wants is a crucial skill for managing your money wisely.

Before you make a purchase, ask yourself if it is something you truly need or if it's just something you want in the moment. If it is a want, consider whether there are more important things you could do with your money, like saving for a goal or investing for the future.

Understanding the distinction between needs and wants helps you make thoughtful spending choices. It also shows you the value of prioritizing your goals over short-term desires.

By mastering these money basics—earning, saving, spending, setting goals, and understanding needs versus wants—you are building a strong foundation for your financial journey. Investing is like a puzzle, and these pieces are essential for putting it together successfully. With the right knowledge and skills, you are well on your way to becoming a smart investor who knows how to make every dollar count.

In the next chapter, we'll delve deeper into the exciting world of investments, exploring different types of investments and how they work. Just like you're learning about different tools in a toolbox, you're building a toolkit of financial skills that will serve you throughout your life.

Chapter 3. Understanding Different Types of Investments

Investing is like having a toolbox filled with various tools, each designed for a specific purpose. In the world of finance, these tools are called investments. They are the vehicles through which your money can grow and work for you. Let us explore some of the most common types of investments that you can use to build your financial future.

Stocks: Owning a Piece of a Company

Imagine you and your friends decide to start a lemonade stand together. You each put in some money to buy lemons, cups, and a table. In return for your investment, you own a part of the lemonade stand and share in its profits.

Stocks work in a similar way. When you buy a stock, you are buying a tiny piece of a company. Companies sell stocks to raise money for things like expanding their business, developing new products, or hiring more employees. As a shareholder, you are entitled to a portion of the company's profits, called dividends, if the company chooses to pay them.

However, investing in stocks comes with risks. The value of a company's stock can go up or down based on factors like its financial performance, competition, and overall market conditions. It is important to research and choose stocks wisely, diversifying your investments to spread out the risk.

Bonds: Lending Money to Governments and Corporations

Imagine you lend money to a friend, and they promise to pay you back with a little extra as a thank-you. Bonds work in a similar way. When you buy a bond, you are essentially lending money to a government or a corporation. In return, they promise to pay you back the money with interest at a specified future date.

Bonds are generally considered to be less risky than stocks because you are lending to established entities, like governments or well-established companies. However, the amount of interest you earn from bonds may be lower than the potential returns from stocks.

Mutual Funds: Investing in a Basket of Stocks and Bonds

Picture a basket filled with a variety of fruits. Each fruit contributes to the overall flavour and nutrition of the basket. Mutual funds work similarly by bundling together a collection of stocks, bonds, or other assets. When you invest in a mutual fund, you are essentially buying a small piece of the entire collection.

Mutual funds are managed by professionals who decide which assets to include and when to buy or sell. They offer diversification, which means your investment is spread across various companies or bonds, reducing the impact if one investment does not perform well.

Real Estate: Investing in Properties

Imagine you own a house, and you decide to rent it out to someone. They pay you rent each month, and over time, your property might also increase in value. Real estate investing involves buying properties like homes, apartments, or commercial buildings with the goal of generating rental income and potential appreciation.

Investing in real estate can be a great way to diversify your portfolio and create a steady stream of passive income. However, it also requires careful research, management, and maintenance.

Saving Accounts vs. Investing Accounts

Think of a piggy bank where you save your allowance. A savings account is like a digital version of that piggy bank, but it is held at a bank. When you deposit money into a savings account, the bank pays you a small amount of interest in return.

Investing accounts, on the other hand, are designed specifically for investing. These accounts allow you to buy stocks, bonds, mutual funds, and other investments. Investing accounts typically offer the potential for higher returns than savings accounts but also come with more risk.

Understanding the different types of investments is like having a variety of tools in your financial toolbox. Each tool serves a different purpose and comes with its own benefits and risks. As you learn about these tools, you'll become better equipped to make informed decisions about how to grow your money and achieve your financial goals.

In the next chapter, we'll explore the concept of risk and return, helping you understand how to assess the level of risk you're comfortable with and how it relates to the potential rewards of investing. Remember, the more you know, the better you will be at building a strong financial future.

Chapter 4. Risk and Return

Investing is an exciting journey filled with opportunities, but it is important to remember that along with opportunities come risks. In this chapter, we will explore the concepts of risk and return—two crucial elements that every investor should understand.

What is Risk?

Risk is the possibility that your investment might not perform as expected, leading to potential financial loss. Think of it as the uncertainty that comes with investing. Just like you cannot predict the weather with 100% accuracy, you cannot predict exactly how an investment will perform in the future.

Different investments carry different levels of risk. Some investments, like stocks, have a higher potential for growth but also come with greater risk. Other investments, like bonds, tend to be more stable but might offer lower returns.

Understanding Volatility

Imagine riding a roller coaster. It is thrilling, right? But there are moments when the ride dips and turns sharply, making your heart race. Investing can be a bit like a roller coaster ride too, with its ups and downs.

Volatility refers to the degree of variation in an investment's value over time. Investments that experience frequent and large fluctuations in value are considered volatile. Volatile investments can be exciting when they are on the rise, but they can also be nerve-wracking when they are falling.

While volatility can be intimidating, it is also an opportunity. Volatile markets can create chances to buy investments at lower prices, potentially leading to higher returns when the market bounces back.

Risk Tolerance: Finding Your Comfort Zone

Just like some people love extreme sports and others prefer calm activities, investors have different levels of comfort with risk. This comfort level is known as your risk tolerance. It is essential to know how much risk you are willing to take on before you start investing.

To determine your risk tolerance, ask yourself how you would feel if your investment suddenly dropped in value by 20% or more. If the thought makes you anxious, you might have a lower risk tolerance and prefer investments with more stability. If you are more comfortable with the idea of short-term fluctuations, you might have a higher risk tolerance and be open to more volatile investments.

Remember that risk tolerance can change over time, so it is essential to reassess periodically as you gain more experience and your financial goals evolve.

The Relationship Between Risk and Return

Imagine you are offered two paths: one is a smooth, well-paved road, and the other is a rugged, unpaved trail. The well-paved road might be safer, but the rugged trail could lead to breathtaking views. The relationship between risk and return is a bit like this.

Generally, investments with higher potential returns also come with higher levels of risk. Investments that offer lower potential returns tend to be more stable and less risky. This relationship is a fundamental concept in investing. It means that if you want the opportunity for higher returns, you have to be willing to take on more risk.

However, it is crucial to strike a balance that aligns with your risk tolerance and financial goals. Diversification, which involves spreading your investments across different asset classes, can help manage risk. By diversifying, you reduce the impact of a poor-performing investment on your overall portfolio.

In summary, risk and return are interconnected in the world of investing. While the allure of high returns can be tempting, it is important to evaluate your comfort with risk and choose investments that align with your risk tolerance and goals.

As you continue on with your investment journey, remember that knowledge is your best tool for managing risk. The more you understand about different types of investments, market trends, and your own risk tolerance, the better equipped you will be to navigate the ups and downs of the financial world. In the next chapter, we will explore the concept of compound interest—a powerful force that can greatly impact your investment outcomes.

Chapter 5. The Magic of Compound Interest

Have you ever heard the saying "Time is money"? Well, when it comes to investing, time has a unique power—the power of compound interest. In this chapter, we will explore how compound interest works and why it is often called the "eighth wonder of the world."

How Compound Interest Works

Imagine you have a magic money tree that grows at a certain rate each year. The interesting thing is that not only does the tree grow on the money you initially planted, but it also grows on the fruit it has already produced. This process of earning interest on both your initial investment and the interest it earns is called compound interest.

Let us break it down with a simple example. Say you invest $100 in an account that offers a 5% annual interest rate. After the first year, you will earn $5 in interest, bringing your total to $105. In the second year, you will earn 5% on $105, which is $5.25, bringing your total to $110.25.

As the years go by, this cycle continues, and your money grows faster and faster.

Starting Early: The Biggest Advantage

Now, here is where things get really exciting: the earlier you start investing, the more time your money has to benefit from compound interest. This is why many financial experts emphasize the importance of starting to invest as early as possible.

Imagine you and a friend each invest $1,000. You start investing at age 20, while your friend starts at age 30. Assuming an annual return of 7%, by the time you are both 60, your investment could grow to around $7,600, while your friend's investment might be around $3,900. That is the power of starting early—the extra time allowed your money to work harder and grow more.

The Rule of 72: Doubling Your Money

Wouldn't it be cool if you could predict how long it takes for your money to double? Well, there is a simple rule that can help you estimate that. It is called the Rule of 72.

Here is how it works: Divide 72 by the annual interest rate you expect to earn. The result is roughly the number of years it will take for your money to double. For example, if you expect an average annual return of 8%, your money will take about 9 years (72 ÷ 8) to double.

Using the Rule of 72, you can see the incredible impact of compound interest. If you start with $1,000 and it takes 9 years to double, you will have $2,000. In another 9 years, it will double again to $4,000. And in yet another 9 years, it will double once more to $8,000.

Understanding the power of compound interest is like having a crystal ball that shows you the potential future of your money. It is not magic—it is math. And the earlier you start, the more time your money work its magic.

In the next chapter, we will discuss how to get started with investing and lay the foundation for your investment journey. Remember, even small steps taken early on can lead to significant financial rewards down the road. By harnessing the magic of compound interest, you are setting yourself up for a bright financial future.

Chapter 6. Getting Started with Investing

You have learned about the power of compound interest, and now it is time to put that knowledge into action. In this chapter, we will explore the practical steps to take when getting started with investing.

Open a Custodial Account with a Parent or Guardian

Since you are a kid, you might be wondering how you can actually start investing. The answer lies in custodial accounts. A custodial account is a special type of account that is set up by a parent or guardian on your behalf. They manage the account until you reach the age of majority, which is usually 18 or 21, depending on where you live.

Custodial accounts come in various forms, including brokerage accounts and individual retirement accounts (IRAs). These accounts allow you to buy and sell investments just like any other investor, but with the oversight of your parent or guardian. It is a way to begin your investment journey even before you're old enough to handle the accounts on your own.

Researching Investments: Company Performance, Trends, and News

Investing is not about blindly throwing your money at random investments. It is about making informed decisions based on research and understanding. Before you invest in a company's stock or any other investment, take the time to research it.

Look into the company's financial performance, including its revenue, earnings, and growth trends. Investigate the industry it operates in and consider the company's position within that industry. Analyse news and trends that could impact the company's future prospects.

There are numerous resources available for research, including financial news websites, company annual reports, and investment research platforms. Learning how to evaluate investments based on data and analysis will give you the confidence to make smart choices.

Diversification: Don't Put All Your Eggs in One Basket

Imagine you have a basket with delicate eggs. If you drop the basket, all the eggs might break. But what if you had several baskets, each with a few eggs? If one basket falls, you will still have some intact eggs left. This concept applies to investing too—it is called diversification.

Diversification involves spreading your investments across different types of assets, industries, and geographic regions. The goal is to reduce the risk of a significant loss if one investment performs poorly. When you diversify, you are not putting all your eggs in one basket.

For example, instead of investing all your money in one company's stock, you could spread your investments across different companies and industries. You might also include bonds or other types of assets in your portfolio. Diversification helps balance the potential for higher returns with the aim of minimizing overall risk.

Building Your First Investment Portfolio

As a young investor, your first investment portfolio does not need to be complex. Start with a few carefully chosen investments that align with your research and risk tolerance. Consider including a mix of stocks and bonds to achieve a balance between growth and stability.

Keep in mind that investing is a long-term endeavour. While it can be exciting to watch the ups and downs of the market, it is important to stay focused on your goals and not get swayed by short-term fluctuations.

As you gain experience and confidence, you can continue to learn and refine your investment strategies. Regularly review your portfolio, consider adjusting your investments if your goals change, and stay up-to-date with market trends and news.

Getting started with investing might feel like taking your first steps into a new adventure. You are armed with knowledge about the importance of compound interest, the value of research, and the wisdom of diversification. By opening a custodial account, conducting thorough research, and building a diversified portfolio, you are setting the stage for a successful investment journey.

Remember, investing is a journey of learning and growth. It is okay to start small, make mistakes, and learn along the way. With time, patience, and the right strategies, you will become a savvy investor who is well on their way to achieving their financial goals. In the next chapter, we will explore different investment strategies that can help you make the most of your investments and build a strong financial future.

Chapter 7. Investment Strategies for Kids

Now that you're on your way to building your investment portfolio, it's time to delve deeper into the strategies that can help you make the most of your investments. In this chapter, we'll explore different investment approaches that you can adopt to achieve your financial goals.

Long-Term vs. Short-Term Investing

Investing is like planting a tree. If you keep digging it up to see if it's growing, it won't have a chance to grow tall and strong. Similarly, constantly buying and selling investments in the short term can prevent your money from benefiting fully from the power of compound interest.

Long-term investing involves holding onto your investments for an extended period, often years or even decades. This approach allows your money to weather the ups and downs of the market, potentially leading to more substantial growth over time. Long-term investors focus on the bigger picture and are not swayed by short-term market fluctuations.

On the other hand, short-term investing, also known as trading, involves buying and selling investments quickly to take advantage of short-lived price movements. While it can be exciting, short-term investing requires a deep understanding of market trends, constant monitoring, and can be riskier compared to long-term investing.

As a young investor, focusing on long-term investing can be a smart approach. By holding onto your investments through market cycles, you give your money the time it needs to benefit from compound interest and potentially achieve significant growth.

Dollar-Cost Averaging: Smoothing Out Market Volatility

Remember the roller coaster analogy from earlier? Market volatility is like the ups and downs of that roller coaster ride. While it can be thrilling, it can also be nerve-wracking. Dollar-cost averaging (DCA) is a strategy that can help smooth out the impact of market volatility on your investments.

DCA involves investing a fixed amount of money at regular intervals, regardless of market conditions. When prices are high, you will buy fewer shares, and when prices are low, you will buy more shares. Over time, this strategy averages out the cost of your investments.

For example, if you decide to invest $100 every month in a certain stock, you will buy more shares when the price is low and fewer shares when the price is high. This way, you are not trying to time the market perfectly, which can be challenging even for experienced investors. DCA helps you take advantage of market fluctuations without the stress of trying to predict the best time to invest.

Reinvesting Dividends and Returns

Imagine you have a money tree that produces not only fruit but also seeds. The fruit represents your investments, and the seeds are the dividends and returns they generate. Reinvesting these dividends and returns can significantly boost the growth of your investments over time.

When you reinvest dividends, you use the money earned from your investments to buy more shares of the same investments. This increases the size of your investment portfolio without you having to add more of your own money. Over time, these reinvestments can lead to exponential growth, especially when combined with the power of compound interest.

Reinvesting returns works similarly. When one of your investments grows in value, you can sell a portion of it and use the proceeds to invest in other opportunities. This way, you are diversifying your portfolio and capitalizing on different growth opportunities.

Tailoring Strategies to Your Goals

As you explore different investment strategies, keep in mind that there is no one-size-fits-all approach. The strategy you choose should align with your goals, risk tolerance, and the amount of time you are willing to commit to managing your investments.

Long-term investing, dollar-cost averaging, and reinvesting dividends and returns are strategies that work well for many investors, especially those who are just starting their investment journey. These strategies help you take advantage of the benefits of time and compounding while minimizing the impact of market volatility.

Ultimately, the key is to be patient and stay focused on your goals. Investing is a marathon, not a sprint, and by adopting thoughtful strategies and allowing your investments to grow over time, you are well on your way to achieving financial success.

In the next chapter, we will delve into the concept of building a winning investment portfolio. We will explore how to balance different types of investments to achieve the right mix of growth potential and risk management. By understanding the art of portfolio construction, you will be equipped to make smart decisions that pave the way for a bright financial future.

Chapter 8. Building a Winning Portfolio

Just like a skilled chef combines various ingredients to create a delicious dish, a successful investor blends different types of investments to create a winning portfolio. In this chapter, we'll explore the art of portfolio construction, along with the importance of regular review and staying informed.

Setting Up a Balanced Portfolio

Imagine you are at a buffet with a variety of foods—vegetables, fruits, proteins, and desserts. To create a well-rounded and nutritious meal, you would choose a little bit of everything. Building an investment portfolio works similarly—you want a mix of different types of investments to achieve your financial goals while managing risk.

A balanced portfolio typically includes a combination of stocks, bonds, and possibly other asset classes like real estate or commodities. Stocks offer growth potential, while bonds provide stability. By diversifying your investments, you reduce the impact of poor performance in one area.

The allocation of your investments—how much you put into stocks versus bonds—depends on factors like your risk tolerance and investment goals. Generally, younger investors might have a higher allocation to stocks, as they have more time to recover from market fluctuations. As you get older, you might gradually shift toward a more conservative allocation.

Regularly Reviewing and Adjusting Your Investments

Think of your investment portfolio as a garden that needs regular care and attention. Just as you would water your plants and remove any weeds, your portfolio requires periodic review and adjustments.

Market conditions, your financial goals, and your risk tolerance can change over time. That is why it is crucial to review your portfolio regularly—maybe once a year or whenever there are significant life changes. During these reviews, ask yourself if your investments are still aligned with your goals and if any adjustments are needed.

For example, if your stocks have performed exceptionally well and now make up a larger portion of your portfolio than intended, you might need to rebalance by selling some stocks and buying more bonds. This process ensures that your portfolio remains in line with your desired allocation and risk level.

Staying Informed: Keeping Up with Financial News

Imagine you are sailing on a ship. To navigate safely, you need to keep an eye on the weather, currents, and other ships. Similarly, to navigate the world of investments, you need to stay informed about financial news, market trends, and economic developments.

Regularly reading financial news, watching market updates, and staying informed about global events can help you make informed decisions. For example, if you are invested in a certain industry and you hear news about new regulations that might impact that industry, you will be better prepared to adjust your investments accordingly.

However, it is important to strike a balance. While staying informed is essential, it is also easy to get overwhelmed by the constant stream of information. Avoid making impulsive decisions based on short-term news fluctuations, and remember that your investment strategy should be aligned with your long-term goals.

Building a winning portfolio requires a combination of art and strategy. Just like an artist selects the right colours to create a masterpiece, you are selecting the right investments to create a financial future that aligns with your dreams and goals.

By setting up a balanced portfolio that matches your risk tolerance and regularly reviewing and adjusting your investments, you are taking proactive steps toward financial success. Staying informed keeps you aware of the ever-changing financial landscape, allowing you to make educated decisions.

In the next chapter, we will explore the concept of ethical investing and social responsibility. You will discover how your investments can align with your values and contribute to a better world. Remember, building a winning portfolio is a journey, and with the right strategies and knowledge, you are well on your way to creating a bright and prosperous financial future.

Chapter 9. Ethical Investing and Social Responsibility

Investing is not just about making money—it is also about making a positive impact on the world. In this chapter, we will explore the concept of ethical investing and how you can align your investments with your values while considering environmental, social, and governance (ESG) factors.

Investing in Companies That Align with Your Values

Imagine you are choosing a team to join. You would want to be part of a team that shares your values and works toward a common goal, right? Investing works in a similar way. You can choose to invest in companies that align with your personal values and beliefs.

Ethical investing, also known as socially responsible investing (SRI) or sustainable investing, involves selecting investments based on both financial considerations and the impact they have on society and the environment. Instead of solely focusing on financial returns, ethical investing takes into account the broader consequences of your investments.

For example, if you care deeply about environmental issues, you might choose to invest in companies that prioritize sustainable practices and work to reduce their carbon footprint. If you value diversity and inclusion, you might seek out companies that promote equal opportunities for all employees.

Environmental, Social, and Governance (ESG) Factors

Ethical investing often centers around what are known as ESG factors—environmental, social, and governance considerations. Let's break down each of these categories:

- Environmental: This involves evaluating a company's impact on the environment. It considers factors like carbon emissions, resource usage, and waste management. Companies that prioritize environmental sustainability might focus on renewable energy, efficient resource utilization, and reduced emissions.

- Social: Social factors encompass a company's treatment of employees, customers, and communities. Companies that value social responsibility might have strong labour practices, diversity and inclusion initiatives, and philanthropic efforts to support communities.

- Governance: Governance refers to a company's leadership, transparency, and ethical standards. Companies with good governance practices have strong leadership, transparent reporting, and policies that promote ethical behaviour.

By considering ESG factors, ethical investors ensure their investments support companies that make positive contributions to society and the planet. Many investment funds and platforms now offer options for ethical investing, allowing you to align your financial choices with your values.

Investing with Impact

Ethical investing goes beyond just avoiding companies that do not align with your values; it is about actively investing in businesses that are making a positive impact. This approach allows you to be a part of the solution and contribute to positive change.

For instance, you might choose to invest in companies that develop renewable energy solutions, improve healthcare access in underserved communities, or promote fair labour practices throughout their supply chains. These investments can generate financial returns while also supporting causes that matter to you.

The Power of Your Investment Choices

Imagine you have a vote in a big decision that affects the world. Your investments are like your vote—they have the power to shape the direction companies take and influence how they operate. By choosing to invest in companies that prioritize sustainability and social responsibility, you are sending a message that these values matter.

Ethical investing allows you to use your financial resources to support positive change, making you not only an investor but also an advocate for a better world. As you continue your investment journey, consider how your choices can contribute to a more sustainable and just future.

Ethical investing and social responsibility are about recognizing that your investments have the potential to create meaningful impact. By aligning your financial choices with your values and considering ESG factors, you are actively participating in building a better future.

In the final chapter, we will wrap up your journey as a young investor. You will reflect on the valuable lessons you have learned, the steps you have taken to grow your knowledge, and the path you're carving toward financial success and a fulfilling life. Remember, every investment you make is a step toward both your financial goals and a world you believe in.

Chapter 10. Avoiding Common Investment Mistakes

Congratulations! You have embarked on an exciting journey as a young investor, armed with knowledge about investing strategies, ethical considerations, and the power of compound interest. As you navigate this journey, it is important to be aware of common investment mistakes and how to avoid them. In this chapter, we will explore some pitfalls to watch out for and the keys to successful investing.

FOMO (Fear of Missing Out) and Emotional Investing

Imagine a carnival with various rides, games, and attractions. If you see a long line forming for a particular ride, you might feel a sense of urgency to join in, fearing you will miss out on the fun. This concept—fear of missing out (FOMO)—also applies to investing.

FOMO can lead to emotional investing decisions, where you make choices based on short-term trends, excitement, or pressure to keep up with others. Emotional investing can cloud your judgment and lead to impulsive decisions that may not align with your long-term goals.

To avoid falling into the FOMO trap, it is crucial to stay grounded and make decisions based on research, analysis, and your well-defined investment strategy. Remember that investing is a marathon, not a sprint, and avoiding emotional reactions is key to maintaining a steady course.

Timing the Market: A Fool's Errand

Imagine trying to predict the exact moment a balloon will pop. It is nearly impossible, right? Timing the stock market is equally challenging. Attempting to buy at the lowest point and sell at the highest point is a strategy that even experienced investors struggle with.

Market timing involves making decisions based on short-term market movements. While it might seem tempting to wait for the "perfect" time to invest, the reality is that even experts cannot consistently predict market fluctuations. Trying to time the market can lead to missed opportunities and increased transaction costs.

Instead of timing the market, focus on time in the market. Invest for the long term and hold onto your investments through market ups and downs. This approach allows you to benefit from the power of compound interest and reduce the impact of short-term market volatility.

Patience and Discipline: The Keys to Success

Imagine you are learning a musical instrument. Progress takes time, practice, and patience. Similarly, successful investing requires patience and discipline. It is about adhering to your investment strategy, even when the market gets turbulent or when you hear about "hot" investment tips.

Patience means giving your investments time to grow and ignoring short-term noise. Discipline means sticking to your investment plan and avoiding impulsive decisions. It is important to remember that investing is a journey that requires both steady commitment and the ability to weather uncertainties.

Developing patience and discipline takes time, but it is an investment in your financial future. Surround yourself with trusted sources of information, follow your well-thought-out investment plan, and resist the urge to make sudden changes based on emotions or market hype.

As you reflect on your journey through this book, you have gained a wealth of knowledge about investing, from understanding compound interest to building a winning portfolio and considering ethical factors. You have discovered the pitfalls to avoid and the strategies that can lead to success.

The keys to successful investing are patience, discipline, and knowledge. By avoiding common mistakes like emotional investing and trying to time the market, you are setting yourself up for a bright financial future. Remember that every decision you make, no matter how small, is a step toward achieving your goals.

Stay curious, continue learning, and do not be afraid to seek advice from trusted mentors or financial professionals. Investing is a lifelong journey, and with the right approach, you are well on your way to building a strong financial foundation that will serve you throughout your life.

As you move forward, remember that you have the power to make a positive impact through your investments. Whether you are growing your own wealth, supporting causes you care about, or aligning with companies that prioritize sustainability, your choices matter.

Congratulations once again on taking the first steps toward becoming a savvy investor. Your financial journey is just beginning, and the world of opportunities is yours to explore.

Chapter 11. Real-Life Stories of Young Investors

Throughout history, young individuals with determination, curiosity, and a knack for investing have managed to achieve remarkable financial success. In this chapter, we will explore inspiring stories of kids and teens who turned their passion for investing into substantial wealth, proving that age is no barrier to achieving financial goals.

Warren Buffett: A Young Investor's Journey to Success

One of the most well-known names in the investing world, Warren Buffett, began his journey as a young investor. At just 11 years old, he made his first investment in the stock market. He purchased three shares of a company for $38 each and sold them later for $40. Although the profit was small, it marked the beginning of his lifelong fascination with investing.

Buffett's story is a testament to the power of learning and patience. As a young boy, he spent hours reading financial books and analysing companies. He focused on value investing—buying undervalued stocks of solid companies and holding onto them for the long term. Over the years, his disciplined approach and commitment to his investment philosophy turned him into one of the richest individuals in the world.

Jaydyn Carr: From Sneaker Resales to Stocks

Jaydyn Carr, a teenager from Texas, found an innovative way to make money from a young age. He began by reselling sneakers, leveraging his knowledge of trends and market demand. However, his interests soon expanded beyond sneakers to stocks.

At the age of 15, Carr decided to use his savings to start investing in the stock market. He invested in well-known companies like Apple and Google, with a focus on long-term growth. Carr's journey is a reminder that you do not need to be an adult to start building a diversified investment portfolio. With curiosity, determination, and a willingness to learn, young investors like Carr can achieve significant financial milestones.

Rachel Fox: From Acting to Active Trading

Rachel Fox is a unique example of a young investor who combined her talents with financial acumen. Known for her acting roles in TV shows and movies, Fox discovered her interest in investing at a young age. She began by observing her father's investment strategies and soon started managing her own portfolio.

What sets Fox apart is her approach to trading. She engages in active trading, which involves making frequent buy and sell decisions. Her trading strategies have garnered attention for their effectiveness. Fox's story highlights the importance of finding an investment approach that aligns with your skills, interests, and goals.

Monty Kapoor: A Teenager's Entrepreneurial Spirit

Monty Kapoor, a teenager from California, found a creative way to invest while also addressing a problem he encountered. When he realized that his friends often forgot their reusable water bottles, he decided to create an innovative solution. Kapoor launched a company that sells reusable water bottles with embedded QR codes, allowing users to earn rewards for refilling their bottles.

Kapoor's entrepreneurial spirit led him to invest the profits from his business into the stock market. His story underscores the potential for young investors to combine business ventures with traditional investing to create a diversified financial portfolio.

These real-life stories of young investors showcase the incredible potential and opportunities that await individuals who dare to step into the world of investing. Whether it is through long-term value investing, active trading, or combining entrepreneurial ventures with investment strategies, young individuals can make a meaningful impact on their financial futures.

As you embark on your own investment journey, remember that age is not a barrier to success. With the right mindset, dedication, and a thirst for knowledge, you can follow in the footsteps of these inspiring young investors and create a path to financial freedom and accomplishment. Your story as a young investor is just beginning, and the possibilities are endless.

Chapter 12. Planning for the Future

As a young investor, you have the power to shape your financial future and realize your dreams. In this chapter, we will explore how investments can help you achieve your future goals, from education and travel to entrepreneurship. We will also discuss the importance of sharing your knowledge and success with others.

Using Investments for Future Goals: Education, Travel, Entrepreneurship

Investments are more than just numbers on a screen—they are tools that can help you turn your dreams into reality. Whether you are dreaming of pursuing higher education, embarking on exciting travel adventures, or starting your own business, investments can play a pivotal role in achieving these goals.

For education: Higher education can be a significant investment, but it is also an investment in yourself and your future. By starting early and contributing regularly to an investment account, you can create a fund that will help cover tuition, books, and other expenses when the time comes.

For travel: Traveling broadens your horizons and provides valuable life experiences. Instead of relying solely on your savings, you can use investments to fund your travels. Setting up a travel fund and consistently contributing to it can help you explore new places and cultures without sacrificing your long-term financial goals.

For entrepreneurship: If you aspire to start your own business, investments can provide the capital you need to turn your ideas into reality. Many successful entrepreneurs began their journeys with investments from family, friends, or angel investors. By understanding the dynamics of raising capital and leveraging your investment knowledge, you can take bold steps toward entrepreneurial success.

Teaching Others: Sharing Your Knowledge and Success

Imagine having a lantern that lights up a dark path for others. As a young investor who's gained knowledge and experience, you have the opportunity to light up the path for others as well. Sharing your investment journey and success stories can inspire and empower those around you.

Consider sharing your insights through blogs, social media, or local community events. By demystifying investing and breaking down complex concepts, you can encourage others to take charge of their financial futures. Empowering your peers and loved ones to start investing early and make informed decisions is a valuable way to give back and make a positive impact.

As you reflect on the lessons and insights gained throughout this book, it is clear that your journey as a young investor is filled with promise and potential. By harnessing the power of compound interest, diversification, and ethical investing, you are setting yourself up for financial success and alignment with your values.

As you plan for your future goals—whether it is pursuing education, exploring the world, or launching your own ventures—remember that investments are tools at your disposal. With patience, discipline, and a clear vision, you can turn your aspirations into achievements.

Your journey does not end here. As you continue to grow, learn, and invest, you will discover new opportunities and adapt your strategies. And do not forget the importance of sharing your journey with others. By inspiring and guiding your peers, you contribute to a generation that is financially savvy, socially responsible, and eager to create positive change.

Your investment journey is a tapestry of experiences, decisions, and milestones. Embrace it with enthusiasm and the understanding that each choice you make has the potential to shape your financial destiny and impact the world around you. Congratulations on your journey as a young investor, and may your future be filled with prosperity, purpose, and fulfilment.

Chapter 13. Glossary of Investment Terms

Investing comes with its own set of terminology that might seem confusing at first. In this chapter, we will provide explanations for key investment concepts and terms, helping you navigate the world of investing with confidence.

Asset Allocation: The distribution of your investments across different types of assets, such as stocks, bonds, and cash. Asset allocation helps manage risk and align your portfolio with your goals and risk tolerance.

Bonds: Debt securities issued by governments or corporations to raise capital. When you buy a bond, you're essentially lending money to the issuer in exchange for periodic interest payments and the return of the bond's face value at maturity.

Compound Interest: The process of earning interest not only on your initial investment but also on the interest that accumulates over time. Compound interest accelerates the growth of your investments.

Diversification: Spreading your investments across different types of assets and industries to reduce risk. Diversification helps protect your portfolio from poor performance in any single investment.

Dividends: Payments made by companies to their shareholders as a portion of their earnings. Dividends provide investors with a steady stream of income.

Exchange-Traded Fund (ETF): An investment fund that's traded on stock exchanges, representing a basket of assets like stocks, bonds, or commodities. ETFs offer diversification and can be bought and sold throughout the trading day.

Index: A collection of securities used as a benchmark to measure the performance of a specific market or investment category. Examples include the S&P 500 and the Dow Jones Industrial Average.

Investment Horizon: The length of time you plan to hold onto your investments. Long-term investments have a horizon of many years, while short-term investments are typically held for less than a year.

Liquidity: The ease with which an investment can be converted into cash without significantly impacting its price. Cash is highly liquid, while real estate might have lower liquidity.

Market Capitalization: The total value of a company's outstanding shares of stock. It's calculated by multiplying the stock price by the number of shares.

Mutual Fund: A pooled investment vehicle managed by professionals that invests in a diversified portfolio of stocks, bonds, or other securities. Mutual funds allow investors to access a range of investments without directly buying individual securities.

Portfolio: A collection of investments owned by an individual or entity. Portfolios can include a mix of stocks, bonds, mutual funds, ETFs, and other assets.

Risk Tolerance: Your ability and willingness to take on risk when investing. It's influenced by factors like your financial situation, goals, and comfort with market fluctuations.

Stocks: Shares of ownership in a company. When you buy stocks, you become a shareholder and have the potential to benefit from the company's growth and profitability.

Volatility: The degree of variation in an investment's price over time. High volatility indicates significant price fluctuations, while low volatility suggests more stable price movements.

Yield: The income generated by an investment, usually expressed as a percentage of its value. For example, the dividend yield of a stock is the annual dividend payment divided by the stock's price.

Chapter 14. Resources for Further Learning

Congratulations on your journey as a young investor! As you continue to expand your knowledge and refine your investment strategies, it is important to have reliable resources at your fingertips. In this chapter, we'll provide a list of books, websites, and online courses that can help you deepen your understanding of investing and personal finance.

Books for Young Investors:

1. "The Motley Fool Investment Guide for Teens" by David Gardner and Tom Gardner: This book introduces the basics of investing in a fun and engaging way, tailored for teenagers. It covers topics like stocks, mutual funds, and building a diversified portfolio.

2. "Growing Money: A Complete Investing Guide for Kids" by Gail Karlitz and Debbie Honig: This comprehensive guide breaks down investment concepts, providing insights into stocks, bonds, and even real estate. It also includes interactive activities to reinforce learning.

3. "Better Than a Lemonade Stand: Small Business Ideas for Kids" by Daryl Bernstein: For young entrepreneurs interested in starting their own ventures, this book offers practical advice and ideas for businesses you can launch as a kid.

Websites and Online Platforms:

1. Investopedia (www.investopedia.com): Investopedia is a comprehensive resource for investment education. It offers articles, tutorials, and explanations of investment terms and concepts.

2. The Motley Fool (www.fool.com): The Motley Fool provides investment advice and insights, tailored for various experience levels. They offer articles, podcasts, and online communities where you can connect with other investors.

3. Khan Academy (www.khanacademy.org): Khan Academy offers free online courses covering a wide range of subjects, including finance and economics. Their investment-related courses can help you understand complex concepts in a simple way.

Online Courses and Learning Platforms:

1. Coursera (www.coursera.org): Coursera offers a variety of courses related to finance and investing. Search for topics like "personal finance," "investment management," and "financial markets" to find relevant courses.

2. Udemy (www.udemy.com): Udemy hosts a diverse range of courses, including those related to investing, trading, and personal finance. Look for courses that align with your interests and learning goals.

3. LinkedIn Learning (www.linkedin.com/learning): Formerly known as Lynda.com, this platform offers video courses on various topics, including finance and investing. You can explore courses on investing strategies, financial planning, and more.

Local Investment Clubs and Meetups:

Check if there are any investment clubs or meetups in your local area. These gatherings provide opportunities to connect with fellow investors, share experiences, and learn from one another's successes and challenges.

Financial Literacy Programs:

Some organizations offer financial literacy programs specifically designed for young individuals. These programs often cover budgeting, saving, investing, and other important financial concepts. Search online or ask your school counselor for recommendations.

Your Local Library:

Do not underestimate the value of your local library. Libraries often have a selection of books, magazines, and resources related to finance and investing. Librarians can help you find relevant materials to support your learning journey.

The world of investing is vast and dynamic, and there is always more to learn. By exploring the books, websites, online courses, and local resources mentioned in this chapter, you are investing in your own education and setting yourself up for financial success.

Remember that investing is a lifelong journey, and continuous learning is a key part of that journey. As you expand your knowledge and apply what you have learned, you'll become a more confident and informed investor. Stay curious, stay motivated, and keep seeking out opportunities to grow your understanding of investing and personal finance. Your dedication to learning will pay off in the long run, helping you make sound financial decisions that shape your future.